AN AFRICAN GOSPEL

AN AFRICAN GOSPEL

Bénédite de la Roncière

Paulist Press
New York / Mahwah, NJ

The Scripture quotations contained herein are the author's translation..

Cover image by Bénédite de la Roncière

Original French edition *L'évangile en pays Mafa* by Bénédite de la Roncière, copyright © 2017 by Editions de l'Emmanuel; 89, Bd Auguste Blanqui – 75013 Paris, France.

Library of Congress Cataloging-in-Publication Data
Names: La Roncière, Bénédite de, author.
Title: An African gospel / Benedite de la Ronciere.
Other titles: Évangile en pays Mafa. English
Description: New York : Paulist Press, 2020. | Summary: "Rediscover the life of Jesus Christ through the landscapes and culture of the Mafa people from North Cameroon, Africa. This gorgeously illustrated book offers an invitation to contemplate anew the message of Christ, and to grasp the reality of a God who came to earth for all people"— Provided by publisher.
Identifiers: LCCN 2019049450 (print) | LCCN 2019049451 (ebook) | ISBN 9780809167937 (paperback) | ISBN 9781587688751 (ebook)
Subjects: LCSH: Jesus Christ. | Mafa (African people)—Religion. | Christianity—Cameroon.
Classification: LCC BT303 .L22513 2020 (print) | LCC BT303 (ebook) | DDC 230.096711—dc23
LC record available at https://lccn.loc.gov/2019049450
LC ebook record available at https://lccn.loc.gov/2019049451

ISBN 978-0-8091-6793-7 (paperback)
ISBN 978-1-58768-875-1 (e-book)

Published by Paulist Press
997 Macarthur Boulevard
Mahwah, New Jersey 07430
www.paulistpress.com

Printed and bound in the United States of America
by Versa Press
Peoria, Illinois
June 2020

Table of Contents

Introduction 1
1. The Annunciation 4
2. The Visitation 6
3. The Birth of Jesus 8
4. The Presentation in the Temple 10
5. The Adoration of the Magi 12
6. The Flight into Egypt 14
7. Jesus and the Teachers 16
8. Jesus in Nazareth 18
9. John the Baptist in the Desert 20
10. The Baptism of Jesus 22
11. The Temptation in the Desert 24
12. The First Two Disciples 26
13. The Wedding at Cana 28
14. Nicodemus 30
15. The Samaritan Woman 32
16. The Miraculous Catch 34

17. The Paralyzed Man 36
18. The Beatitudes 38
19. The Woman Who Loved Greatly 40
20. The Parable of the Sower 42
21. The Hidden Treasure 44
22. The Possessed Boy 46
23. Jesus Calms a Storm 48
24. The Multiplication of Bread 50
25. The Daughter of Jairus 52
26. The Transfiguration 54
27. The Unfaithful Woman 56
28. Jesus Heals the Blind Man 58
29. The Good Samaritan 60
30. The Good Shepherd 62
31. Martha and Mary 64
32. The Persistent Friend 66
33. The Rich Fool 68
34. The Guests at the Feast 70
35. The Parable of the Prodigal Son 72
36. The Rich Man and Poor Lazarus 74
37. The Merciless Servant 76
38. The Ten People with Leprosy 78
39. The Pharisee and the Tax Collector 80
40. Jesus and the Children 82

41. The Workers Who Arrived Last 84
42. The Ten Bridesmaids 86
43. The Raising of Lazarus 88
44. Zacchaeus 90
45. The Parable of the Talents 92
46. Palm Branches 94
47. Jesus Chases Out the Money Changers 96
48. The Widow's Gift 98
49. Jesus Washes Peter's Feet 100
50. The Last Supper 102
51. Gethsemane 104
52. Judas's Kiss 106
53. Peter Denies Jesus 108
54. Jesus Is Scourged 110
55. The Crucifixion 112
56. The Resurrection 114
57. The Women at the Tomb 116
58. Jesus Appears to Mary Magdalene 118
59. On the Way to Emmaus 120
60. Thomas 122
61. Sent on a Mission 124
62. The Ascension of Jesus 126
63. Pentecost 128

Introduction

In 1964, an artist named Bénédite de la Roncière went to Dakar, the capital of Senegal in West Africa, where her husband had taken a job as a teacher. While they lived there, Bénédite wrote and illustrated a children's book called *Assoua: Petit Sénégalais de Casamance* (Assoua: The Little Senegalese Boy from Casamance), which was published in 1969.

Fr. François Vidil, a missionary priest in West Africa, discovered this book. He had been searching for pictures to help him explain the Gospel to the people he served and to show them that the Christian religion was not "just something for white people," but that Jesus had come for everyone. He wanted pictures that showed people a black Christ. He was organizing a competition in several African countries to find an artist to take on such a project and contacted Bénédite about the competition. She entered it and was chosen as the artist for his project.

As a result, Bénédite was invited in 1976 to a village in northern Cameroon, among the people known as the Mafa. There was no electricity, no gas, no running water, and no telephone, and the post office car was broken down. But a warm welcome awaited her. Each morning when she opened her door, thirty children were patiently waiting for her. They scrambled to carry her art supplies and delighted in watching her draw. All the inhabitants of the village helped out in Bénédite's work by staging each of the scenes that she wanted to paint. They took their places as different people in the Gospel stories, and she painted them. Fr. François also invited a group of Cameroonian priests, deacons, and catechists to provide Bénédite with guidance. Should the angels have wings? Should they have halos? What color should Christ's garments be—white, or red like kings wear? Day after day, they collected photos, sketches, and drawings.

The first paintings were printed and used by catechists serving in rural areas of Africa. By 1986, they had at their disposal a collection of sixty images created by Bénédite. They were all published over the following years in the form of postcards, posters, slides, and DVDs. By 2005, six million copies of Bénédite's work had been sold. In 2014, the images of the Mafa Jesus were in ninety-one countries. Throughout this time, Bénédite received letters from people all over the world telling her how much her work delighted and inspired them.

Throughout these pages, *An African Gospel* invites us to discover the life of Jesus Christ in a new way. May this book help us to grasp the reality of a God who comes to earth to meet each and every person, and to show them the infinite love of God.

1 The Annunciation

Luke 1:26–38

God sent the angel Gabriel to a little town in **Galilee** called Nazareth, to a young woman named Mary, who was engaged to be married. Standing before her, Gabriel said, "Hail, Mary. The Lord is with you! You are going to become pregnant and give birth to a baby boy. And you will name him Jesus. He will be great and will be called the Son of God the Most High, and his kingdom will last forever. Your cousin Elizabeth is already pregnant, even though she is past the age when anyone thought she could bear a child. For nothing is impossible with God!"

In the mountains of northern Cameroon, where these scenes were staged, people's homes are made up of several similar huts built in a cluster. Each hut has a specific purpose—one is a kitchen, one is a bedroom, and so on—and each is covered with a pointed roof. They are connected to each other and open onto a small central yard, called a concession, like the one we see here.

In this image, Mary is preparing a meal as God's messenger appears.

Galilee: a province in the northern region of Palestine

2 The Visitation

Luke 1:39–56

Mary got up and hurried to a town in the hill country where her cousin Elizabeth lived with her husband, Zechariah. When Mary arrived, she greeted Elizabeth. As soon as Elizabeth saw Mary, she was filled with the Holy Spirit and cried out, "Blessed are you among women! And blessed is the fruit of your womb! Why is God so good to me, to send the mother of my Lord to visit me? As soon as I heard your voice, the baby inside me jumped for joy!" And Mary said, "My soul gives glory to the Lord! My spirit delights in God my Savior. He has given me, a girl from nowhere, a big place in his plan, and so all people will call me blessed. The Mighty One has done great things for me. His name is holy."

The Mafa people build their homes on hilltops for more security. This landscape is a lot like the hills that Mary traveled to when she went to visit her cousin Elizabeth.

3 The Birth of Jesus

Luke 2:4–21

Mary and Joseph went to **Bethlehem**, but they couldn't find anywhere there to stay. So they rested in a barn, and that's where Mary gave birth to a son. She wrapped her baby boy in blankets and laid him in one of the feed boxes that the farmers used for their animals. In the fields nearby, there were shepherds looking after their sheep. An angel of the Lord appeared to them, wrapped in God's glory. The shepherds were terrified, but the angel said, "Don't be afraid. I bring you joyful news for the whole world! Today in Bethlehem, a Savior has been born for you. He is **Christ** the Lord."

The Mafa build shelters in the fields where they can store their crops so that they are out of reach of wild animals. This is where the shepherds find Mary, Joseph, and the newborn Jesus.

Bethlehem: a town in Palestine
Christ: anointed, which means to be made sacred by God; Christ in Hebrew is "Messiah"

4 The Presentation in the Temple

Luke 2:22–38

Joseph and Mary took baby Jesus to the temple, a sacred building in Jerusalem where God dwelled in a special way. There was a holy man inside named Simeon, who was led by the Holy Spirit. When he saw Jesus, Simeon lifted the baby up in his arms and praised God, saying, "Lord, you are the King. I see that the salvation you promised has now come, a light to the whole world. Now I, your servant, can go in peace."

Another holy person in the temple was a prophet named Anna. She spent all her days and nights there, worshiping and praying to God. When Anna saw Jesus and his family, she gave thanks to God and began telling everyone, "The time has come for God's people to be set free!"

Joseph brings two doves to the temple as offerings to God. The prophet Anna approaches to look at the child. The temple is shown in an African building style, using earth and wooden beams, and the floor is lined with mats.

5 The Adoration of the Magi

Matthew 2:1–12

After Jesus was born, wise men from far away arrived in Jerusalem, saying, "We saw a star in the sky that led us here. We are looking for the newborn child who will someday be king of the Jews. We have come to worship him." When Herod, the king of that region, heard about this, he became angry and scared. So he called together all the religious leaders and he asked them where the Messiah was supposed to be born. "In the town of Bethlehem," they told him. So King Herod summoned the wise men and sent them to look for the child in Bethlehem. "As soon as you find him, let me know, because I want to go and worship him, too," he said.

The wise men went joyfully, led by the amazing star, until they found Jesus with Mary and Joseph in Bethlehem. They bowed down and worshiped Jesus, and they laid gifts before him—gold, incense, and myrrh. Before they left, God told them in a dream not to go back to King Herod. So they went back home a different way.

The wise men from far away have just arrived to visit Mary, Joseph, and Jesus. Tradition tells us their names are Melchior, Balthazar, and Caspar. As they present their gifts, a servant fans them, while two young children play music for Jesus. Behind the group, their caravan rests in the shade of the trees. Meanwhile, in Jerusalem, Herod plans to kill this child because he is afraid Jesus will someday take away Herod's power.

6 The Flight into Egypt

Matthew 2:13–14

After the wise men left Bethlehem, an angel of the Lord appeared to Joseph in a dream. The angel told Joseph, "King Herod is going to try to kill Jesus. Get up and go with Mary and the baby, and escape to Egypt, where it will be safe." That very night, the family left for Egypt.

The Holy Family *escapes* into the night to get away from King Herod. They will not go back home until after the king dies.

7 Jesus and the Teachers

Luke 2:41–50

Every year all the Jewish people who were able—including Mary, Joseph, and Jesus—went to Jerusalem to celebrate the feast of **Passover**. When Jesus was twelve years old, they went again. But this time, after they had celebrated the feast and were returning to Nazareth where they lived, Jesus stayed behind in Jerusalem without his parents noticing. They had thought he was with one of the other families traveling in their caravan!

When they realized Jesus was missing, they were terrified and hurried back to Jerusalem to search for him. Finally, after three days, they found him! He was inside the holy temple, sitting with the Jewish **teachers** and talking with them about God. Everyone who heard Jesus talk about God was amazed at what he said.

The teachers are amazed. They thought they knew more about God than anyone else, but here is a twelve-year-old child who shows that he knows as much as them, and more!

Scrolls like the one in the picture were hidden centuries ago in caves on the edge of the Dead Sea, in a place called Qumran. Two thousand years later, shepherds discovered them, and now we can read them.

Passover: the great Jewish holy day celebrating the Israelites' escape from slavery in Egypt
Teachers: Jewish scholars who were experts in the holy books; sometimes they are called scribes or doctors of the Law

8 Jesus in Nazareth

Luke 2:51–52

Jesus went back with his parents to Nazareth. There he continued to grow up to be good and wise and strong. As his mother Mary watched him grow, she treasured it all in her heart.

This short passage written by Luke is all we have that tells us about the thirty years that Jesus lived with Joseph and Mary, growing up and learning, and working with Joseph as a carpenter.

9 John the Baptist in the Desert

Matthew 3:1–12 / Mark 1:2–8 / Luke 3:1–21 / John 1:19–28

A man called John the Baptist came to the desert in the region where Jesus lived. He wore clothes made of camel's hair, and he only ate locusts and wild honey. He cried out to everyone, "Turn away from your sins! The kingdom of heaven is coming!" Many centuries earlier, the prophet Isaiah was talking about John when he said, "Someone is shouting in the desert, 'Clear a path, make a road, for God to arrive!'" People from all over came to listen to John preach. They confessed their sins and he baptized them in the Jordan River.

Notice that many of the people listening to John in this picture look pretty unhappy. That is because he is very hard on them! He calls them **hypocrites** and children of snakes, and he compares them to trees that will be cut down and burned when they don't grow good fruit. In fact, he says the ax is already sitting at their trunk, ready to be used.

Water cleans what is dirty. Water is used in baptism to help us understand the forgiveness people receive when they come to confess their sins and let them be washed away.

hypocrites: phony people in the Gospels who insisted on making others do hard things to earn God's love—things that they wouldn't even do themselves; they also focused more on the sins of others instead of their own sins

10 The Baptism of Jesus

Matthew 3:13–17 / Mark 1:9–11 / Luke 3:21–22 / John 1:29–34

While John was baptizing people in the Jordan River, Jesus went to the river and stood in line to be baptized too. John realized who Jesus was and said to him, "I should not be baptizing you. You should be baptizing me!" But Jesus said, "This is the way that God wants it to happen." So John baptized Jesus in the river.

As soon as Jesus came up out of the water, heaven opened up and the Spirit of God came down like a dove above him. Then from heaven, the Father's voice said, "This is my own dear Son, whom I love."

John hesitated to baptize Jesus because he believed he didn't need it. But Jesus wants to give this example of humility to us all.

11 The Temptation in the Desert

Matthew 4:1–11 / Mark 1:12–13 / Luke 4:1–13

After his baptism, Jesus was led by the Holy Spirit into the desert, where the devil tempted him. The devil brought Jesus to the top of a tall mountain and pointed out all the awesome kingdoms of the world. He told Jesus, "If you bow down and worship me, I will give you all of this." And Jesus replied, "Get away from me, Satan! Scripture says, 'Worship and serve God alone'!" So the devil left Jesus alone.

Standing beside Jesus, Satan points toward the landscape below. We see the mountains of northern Cameroon on the horizon. The plains lie before them, with fields, huts, flocks, and the people who live there. The **millet** is already harvested and the stalks are drying, soon to be used as fuel. The artist does not show the devil to be a scary or ugly person. Instead, he is a nice-looking man who tries to make evil look good to people.

Millet: a kind of grain grown for food in Cameroon and many other parts of the world

12 The First Two Disciples

John 1:35–39

While John the Baptist was standing with two of his disciples, they saw Jesus walking by. John pointed to Jesus and said, "Look! There is the Lamb of God!" So the two disciples of John followed after Jesus. Jesus turned around, saw them there, and asked, "What do you want?" "**Rabbi**, where are you staying?" they asked. Jesus replied, "Come and see." So they went along and spent the rest of the day with Jesus.

We see near the men an unfinished hut under construction. For the artist, it symbolizes the beginning of the Christian church: the two disciples of John who became the first of Jesus's apostles (soon there will be twelve), then the crowds that will follow Jesus, and now the hundreds of millions of Christians spread all over the Earth.

John has already proclaimed it, and he says it again: Christ is like a lamb, pure and gentle. He is also, above all, the lamb that will be sacrificed for the sake of the whole world.

Rabbi: means "teacher" in Hebrew

13 The Wedding at Cana

John 2:1–11

There was a wedding in a town called Cana. Jesus and Mary, along with Jesus's disciples, were all invited. During the banquet, the wine ran out and Jesus's mother came to him and said, "There is no wine left." And Jesus replied, "Woman, what does this have to do with me? It is not yet my time." But Mary said to the servers, "Do whatever he tells you."

Jesus pointed out six big stone water jugs; each one could hold thirty gallons. He told the servers to fill them with water. When they had, he told them to bring some to the man in charge of the banquet. So they did, and when the man in charge tasted it, he smiled and said, "You saved the best wine for last!" The water was changed into wine!

The groom, sitting with his new wife among the musicians, has already drunk all the wine from his **calabash**. He asks for more, and the guests around him do, too. As a servant pours the last drop from a jug into the father of the family's calabash, he says, "This is all that's left." It is a white drop because in Cameroon they drink palm wine, made from the delicious sap of the palm tree. The father is upset. He is thinking, "We need more wine! This is embarrassing."

Mary understands. She intervenes because she already knows that her son is sent by God. She is sure of it. This was Jesus's first miracle and it helped his disciples believe in him.

Calabash: a bowl made from the hollow shell of a gourd used to hold and serve liquid

14 Nicodemus

John 3:1–21

There was a **Pharisee** named Nicodemus. He came to Jesus at night and said, "We know that you are a teacher who has come from God, because you could never do the amazing things you are doing if you weren't." Jesus told Nicodemus, "God loved the world so much that he gave his only Son, so that anyone who believes in him would not die but have eternal life. God did not send his Son into the world to condemn the world, but to save the world."

Nicodemus is afraid that other Pharisees who don't like Jesus will see them talking together. He has waited until after dark to go and speak with him. In this picture, they are sitting in the upper loft of a house, where the Mafa store their millet and other crops.

Pharisee: a member of a Jewish group that demanded following the Law very literally and closely, no matter how hard it became to do it

15 The Samaritan Woman

John 4:6–26

On his way back to Galilee, Jesus stopped with his disciples in a town in Samaria called Sychar. He was tired and thirsty, so while his disciples went into town to get some food, Jesus sat down at a well. As he was sitting there, a **Samaritan** woman came to get some water.

"Can I have a drink?" Jesus asked her.

She said, "You're a Jew. I'm a Samaritan and a woman. Why are you asking me for a drink?"

Jesus told her, "If you understood the gift God is offering you and who is sitting here asking you for a drink, you would be asking me for living water, with which you would never be thirsty again."

The woman said, "Sir, please give me this water, so I won't need to keep coming back to this well."

"Go get your husband and come back here," Jesus said.

"I don't have a husband," the woman said.

"I know," Jesus said. "You have had five husbands, and the man you are with now is not your husband."

"Sir, I can see you are a **prophet**," she said. "I know that the Messiah is coming, the Anointed One, and when he comes, he will explain everything."

Jesus said to her, "I'm the one you're talking about."

Ignoring the customs of his day, Jesus speaks to everyone as friends—even to women, and even to this woman who is both a rejected wife and also from Samaria.

Among the Mafa, just as in the time of Jesus, it is the women who go to the well to do the chore of gathering water.

Samaritan: a person from Samaria; Samaritans had different beliefs about God than the Israelites, so the two groups hated and avoided each other
Prophet: someone who boldly proclaims God's word and God's desires for people, denounces sins, and points toward the future

16 The Miraculous Catch

Luke 5:1–11 / John 21:4–14

One day Jesus was teaching the word of God to a large crowd of people near a big lake. His friend Simon Peter's fishing boat was sitting there while Simon cleaned his nets. Jesus got into Simon's boat and said to him, "Go out into deep water and lower your nets to catch some fish."

Simon replied, "Teacher, we have worked hard all night and haven't caught a thing. But if you say so, I will lower the nets." When he did, he caught so many fish that his nets were beginning to rip, and he had to ask his friends in another boat to come and help him. Both boats became so full of fish they nearly sunk! When Simon Peter saw this, he fell before Jesus and said, "You shouldn't be near me, Lord, because I'm a sinful man."

Jesus said to Simon, "Do not be afraid. From now on, you will be catching people."

Simon Peter knows a lot about being a fisherman, and he knows that there were not supposed to be any fish where Jesus told him to find them. So he is amazed by Jesus. Back on the shore, he gives up everything to follow Jesus.

We see two canoes, each cut from the trunk of a tree. Boats like these are still used all the time by many people in parts of Africa. Jesus also used fishing boats to preach to crowds that gathered on the shore.

17 The Paralyzed Man

Matthew 9:1–8 / Mark 2:1–12 / Luke 5:17–26

One day Jesus was teaching the word of God in a house in Capernaum, and so many people came to hear him that there was no more room left in the house. Four men brought their paralyzed friend to see Jesus, but since they could not get near him, they made a hole in the roof above him and lowered their friend down on a mat. When Jesus saw their faith, he said to the man, "Son, your sins are forgiven."

Some of the religious teachers who were standing there thought, "How can this man talk like that? He is **blaspheming.** No one but God can forgive sins!" Jesus knew exactly what they were thinking, so he asked them, "Which would be easier—to tell this man his sins are forgiven, or to tell him to get up and walk? I want you to know that the Son of Man has authority to forgive sins." And he turned to the paralyzed man and said, "Get up. Pick up your mat and go home." And as all the people watched, the man got up, picked up his mat, and walked away. Everyone was amazed and praised God.

While the startled crowd watches, Jesus performs a beautiful miracle of healing. The paralyzed young man feels life returning to his legs. Through the hole in the roof, we see the hand of one of the man's friends, still holding the rope they used to lower him down. Joy breaks out on all the faces of the people gathered around.

Jesus gives proof of his merciful power. Miracles like these helped people to listen to, welcome, and follow him.

Blaspheming: speaking insultingly about God; this was a very serious crime in Jesus's day.

18 The Beatitudes

Matthew 5:1–12 / Luke 6:20–26

A large crowd gathered around Jesus, so he went up the side of a mountain, sat down, and began to teach them. He said,

"Blessed are people who are poor in spirit, for the kingdom of heaven belongs to them.

"Blessed are people who are sad, for they will be comforted.

"Blessed are people who are humble, for they will be given the land.

"Blessed are people who hunger and thirst for what is right, for they will be satisfied.

"Blessed are people who show mercy, for they will receive mercy.

"Blessed are people whose hearts are pure, for they will see God.

"Blessed are people who make peace, for they will be called children of God.

"Blessed are people who suffer for doing what is right, for the kingdom of heaven belongs to them.

"Blessed are you when people insult you and hurt you and say terrible things about you because of me. Rejoice and be happy, for you will receive a great reward in heaven. They did the same thing to the prophets who lived long ago."

Many different kinds of people came to listen to Jesus. We see disabled people, like the beggar dressed in rags and missing one leg. We see an old man weeping for joy, while a child looks at him with surprise. There are babies carried by their mothers or sisters and many purehearted children. Those who suffer, those who struggle against injustice, misery, and hatred, are comforted by these words of Jesus.

19 The Woman Who Loved Greatly

Luke 7:36–50

A Pharisee named Simon invited Jesus to supper at his house and Jesus went. While they were sitting at Simon's table, a woman came in carrying a beautiful bottle full of perfumed oil. Everyone who lived in the town knew she was a sinful woman. She kneeled in front of Jesus, crying, and began to wash his feet with her tears. Then she dried his feet with her long hair, kissed them, and poured precious oil over them. Simon sat there thinking to himself, "If Jesus were really a prophet, he would know what a sinful person this is, touching him like this."

Jesus knew what he was thinking and said, "Simon, do you see this woman? When I came into your house, you didn't offer me water to wash my feet, but she is washing them with her tears and wiping them with her hair. You didn't welcome me with a kiss, but she hasn't stopped kissing my feet since she came in. Simon, all her many sins are forgiven, which is why she shows such great love." Then Jesus turned to the woman and told her, "Your faith has saved you. Go in peace."

20 The Parable of the Sower

Matthew 13:1–23 / Mark 4:1–20 / Luke 8:4–15

Jesus taught the people with parables. Once he said, "A farmer went out to his fields to plant his seeds. As he did, some of the seeds fell on the walking path; they got walked on and birds ate them. Some seeds fell on rocky ground; they started to grow, but they died soon because they didn't get enough water. Some seeds fell among thorn bushes, and the thorns grew up around them and choked them. But some seeds fell on good soil, and when they grew, they produced lots of good crops."

Then Jesus explained what his **parable** meant. "The seeds are the word of God. The seeds on the path stand for people who have heard the word, but then the devil comes and snatches it from their hearts so that they don't believe it. The seeds that fall on rocky ground stand for people who hear God's word and receive it with joy, but the word doesn't take root in their hearts; they believe for a while but forget about it when things get hard. The seeds that fall among thorns stand for people who hear God's word, but as time goes on, their faith is choked off by the worries and money and pleasures of life, and so they don't really grow. But the seeds that fell on good soil stand for people with good and honest hearts who hear the word of God and nourish it in their hearts and remain faithful. They produce a good crop of faith for God."

In this picture, three workers till the ground with their hoes, which are called *daba*. Someone is bringing them water to drink because it is very hot. The small birds that peck at the edge of the path are called cardinals because of their red feathers, red like the special clothes worn by cardinals, the pope's closest advisors.

Parable: a story told by Jesus to help him explain something to the people he taught

21 The Hidden Treasure

Matthew 13:44

Jesus told this little parable: "The kingdom of heaven is like a treasure that was buried in a field. A man found it there and then hid it again. Filled with joy, he went and sold everything he owned and used all of the money to buy that field, so he could have the treasure."

Here, the farmer has his two oxen hitched to a yoke that they use to pull the plow. While plowing, he suddenly feels the blade of his plow strike something. He digs with his *daba* to figure out what is down there and discovers—treasure! Discovering the treasure of the word of God can change our lives like the treasure in the parable will change this farmer's life.

22 The Possessed Boy

Matthew 17:14–20 / Mark 9:14–29 / Luke 9:37–43

A man came with his son to Jesus and said, “Teacher, this is my son. He is possessed by a spirit that takes hold of him and throws him to the ground. He foams at the mouth and grinds his teeth and his body becomes stiff. If you can do anything, then please have mercy on us and help us.”

Jesus said to him, “Why do you say ‘*if* you can’? Everything is possible to someone who believes.”

The man cried out, “I do believe! Help my lack of faith!”

Then Jesus ordered the unclean spirit to leave the boy and it came out of him.

The roofs of the Mafa houses are not very heavy, so they can be repaired and replaced easily. With time and rain, they will become damaged and gray.

A crowd gathers around the child as he rolls on the ground during a seizure. His father reaches out to him, his mother joins her hands in sadness and despair—and Jesus heals him.

23 Jesus Calms a Storm

Matthew 8:23–27 / Mark 4:35–41 / Luke 8:22–25

One evening, Jesus said to his disciples, "Let's go across to the other side of the lake." They left the crowd, got into a boat, and began to sail across. A big storm came up. The wind blew hard and waves were crashing into the boat, nearly making it sink. Meanwhile, Jesus was in the back of the boat, asleep on a pillow. The disciples woke him up and said, "Teacher, we're about to drown! Don't you care?" He got up and ordered the wind and the waves, "Quiet! Be still!" The wind died down and the lake became calm. Then he asked the disciples, "Why are you so scared? Don't you have any faith?" They were amazed and said to each other, "Who is this person? Even the wind and the waves obey him!"

In the time of Jesus, the Lake of Gennesaret (or Tiberias), in the Jordan Valley, was also called the Sea of Galilee because it is very large, over sixty square miles!

24 The Multiplication of Bread

Matthew 14:13–21 / Mark 6:30–44 / Luke 9:10–17 / John 6:1–13

One day, many people from all over gathered to hear Jesus teach, until there was a crowd of about five thousand people. When Jesus saw the huge crowd, his heart ached for them because they were like sheep without a shepherd. It started to get late and his disciples said to Jesus, "They're all hungry. Send them away so they can go find something to eat in the villages nearby."

"You give them some food," Jesus replied.

They objected, "It would cost eight months of a person's pay to buy enough food for everyone here! You want us to do that?"

"How much food is here now?" Jesus asked.

"We have five loaves of bread and two fish," they said.

Jesus had everyone sit down. He took the bread and the fish, looked up to heaven, and gave thanks to God. Then he told his disciples to pass out the food. Everyone who was there ate until they were full, and there were even twelve baskets of food left over.

The landscape of Palestine was rarely green, just like the Mafa region in the dry season. But there is grass near the lake, and as the crowd gathered around Jesus to hear him teach, he encouraged them to lie down comfortably. Dressed in the traditional, handwoven white garments of the Mafa, the apostles go from one group to another with their large baskets of bread. In this way, Jesus makes sure everyone there gets something to eat. Later, he'll do this in a different and even more special way in the Eucharist.

25 The Daughter of Jairus

Matthew 9:18–26 / Mark 5:21–43 / Luke 8:40–56

An important Jewish man named Jairus came to Jesus and begged him, "My little girl is dying. Please come and lay your hands on her so that she will get better." Jesus went with the man, but before they reached his house, a messenger reached them and said, "Jairus, your daughter has died. There is no need to bother the teacher any longer." But Jesus told him, "Do not be afraid. Just have faith."

When they got to Jairus's house, Jesus saw the family crying and upset. He said to them, "Why are you all so upset? The little girl isn't dead. She's just sleeping." And they were angry at him for saying that.

Jesus took the child's parents to where the girl was, and he said to her, "Little girl, get up." And immediately, the twelve-year-old girl got up and began to walk around. Jesus then told her parents to give her some food.

The girl's parents are crying. A disciple sits nearby, holding on to hope. Jesus looks at the girl tenderly, calling out to her—and the miracle happens!

26 The Transfiguration

Matthew 17:1–9 / Mark 9:2–10 / Luke 9:28–36

Jesus took Peter, James, and John up a high mountain. Suddenly, Jesus was transfigured before them: his face shined like the sun and his clothes became white as light. Moses and Elijah appeared there, too, talking with Jesus. Then a bright cloud surrounded them, and a voice came from the cloud saying, "This is my beloved Son. Listen to him."

When the disciples heard this, they fell on their faces to the ground in fear. But Jesus came and touched them, saying, "Get up, and do not be afraid." And when the disciples looked up again, there was no one there but Jesus. As they walked back down the mountain with him, Jesus told them, "Do not tell anyone about what you just saw until the Son of Man has been raised from the dead."

27 The Unfaithful Woman

John 8:2–11

The religious leaders came to Jesus with a woman who had just been caught cheating on her husband. They said to him, "Teacher, the Law of Moses says that a woman who commits this sin should be **stoned** to death. What do you say?" They were trying to catch him in a trap because they wanted to have something to accuse him of.

Jesus bent down and wrote on the ground with his finger. Then he stood up and said, "Which of you here has never sinned? He should be the one to throw the first stone at her." Then he bent down and wrote on the ground again. While he waited, the men dropped their stones and walked away quietly, one by one, until there was no one left standing there but Jesus and the woman.

"Where did everyone go?" he asked her. "Is no one left to condemn you?"

"No one," the woman said.

"I don't condemn you either," he said. "Now go, and do not sin anymore."

What did Jesus write on the ground? Some think that Jesus was writing the sins of the men and, afraid of seeing their own sins revealed by him, they quickly slipped away. Other people think that the point here is that Jesus writes in the sand, since a marking made in the sand doesn't remain for long. It disappears with the slightest gust of wind. Maybe Jesus wanted to show how easily the breath of divine mercy can erase sins, even the one the woman was accused of. But far from approving of what she had done, Jesus tells her, "Go and sin no more."

Stoning: the awful practice of killing a person with stones

28 Jesus Heals the Blind Man

John 9:1–7

Jesus passed by a man who had been blind since he was born. His disciples asked him, "Teacher, why was this man born blind? Was it because his parents sinned or because he sinned?"

"Neither," Jesus answered. "It was so that people could see God working through him." And then he spat on the ground to make some mud and put it on the man's eyes. Then he told the man to go wash his face in a nearby pool. So the man went and washed, and when he came back, he could see!

Some of the Pharisees did not want to believe the miracle they saw with their own eyes. After the blind man was healed, they insulted him and drove him away. Later, Jesus came to him and said, "I have come into this world so that those who do not see can see."

29 The Good Samaritan

Luke 10:29–37

When Jesus taught that we should love our neighbors, a teacher of the Law asked Jesus, "But who is my neighbor?"

Jesus answered with another parable. He said, "Once a man was traveling from Jerusalem to Jericho, and he was attacked by bandits. They took his clothes, they beat him half to death, and they left him lying on the side of the road. A priest came walking down that road, and when he saw the poor man lying there, he crossed to the other side and kept on going. Then a **Levite** came along, and when he saw the man, he passed by, too. Then, a Samaritan came along, and he saw the man and felt very bad for him. He went to him, cleaned his wounds, and put bandages on him. Then he lifted the man on his donkey, brought him to an inn, and took care of him. Which of these three people do you think was the neighbor to the man who was attacked by bandits?"

The teacher of the Law answered, "The one who treated him with mercy."

Jesus said to him, "Go and act as he did."

There are mountains between Jerusalem and Jericho, just like there are mountains in Cameroon.

Seeing the wounded man, the travelers hurried on, afraid that what happened to him could happen to them, too.

Levite: a worker at the temple of Jerusalem who assisted the priests

30 The Good Shepherd

John 10:1–16

Jesus said, "I am the good shepherd. I know my sheep and my sheep know me, just like the Father knows me and I know the Father. I will give up my life for my sheep. I have other sheep that do not belong to this pasture. I want them to follow me also. They will hear my voice, and there will be one flock and one shepherd."

Here we see the shepherd and his sheep during the dry season in the Mandara Mountains in Cameroon. There has been no rain, so the sheep can only find the remains of the millet stalks after the grain has already been harvested. The millet is piled up on a drying rack near the huts with pointed roofs.

31 Martha and Mary

Luke 10:38–42

While traveling with his disciples, Jesus came to a village where his friends Martha and Mary lived, and he stopped at their house. While he visited, Mary sat at the Lord's feet listening to him, while Martha was busy making Jesus feel welcome. Martha said to him, "Lord, don't you care that my sister has left me to do the serving by myself? Tell her to help me." The Lord said to her, "Martha, Martha, you are worried and upset about many things. But only one thing is important. What Mary has chosen is better, and it will not be taken away from her."

To prepare for a special guest in a Mafa home, you start by grinding millet in a mortar, then cooking and serving it in little round balls of sticky dough called *fufu*. This is the daily food of the people living in this region. *Fufu* is served with a tasty herb sauce. In this image, Martha simmers the food in a pot over a fire built between clay mounds in the hearth.

32 The Persistent Friend

Luke 11:5–10

Jesus said, "Imagine that you go to a friend in the middle of the night and you say, 'Could you lend me three loaves of bread? A friend of mine has just arrived at my house to stay with me, and I have nothing to give him to eat.' And they tell you in reply, 'Don't bother me. My door is locked and we're all in bed. I can't give you anything now.' But I'll tell you, if you keep asking, they will get up and give you something, if not because you are friends, then just to get you to stop asking.

"So remember: Ask and you will receive. Seek and you will find. Knock and the door will be opened for you."

For light at night, the Mafa people use kerosene lamps like the one the persistent friend in the image is holding.

33 The Rich Fool

Luke 12:16–21

Jesus told this parable to the crowd of people listening to him. "There was a rich man whose fields produced a great harvest. He thought, 'I don't have enough space to store my harvest. But I know what I'll do. I'll tear down my barns and build bigger ones. And then I'll have enough good things for a long time. I can relax. I can eat and drink as much as I want. I can enjoy life!'

"But," Jesus continued, "God said to him, 'You fool! This very night you will die. What good will all your things do you now?' This is how it will be for someone who collects riches for himself but forgets the things that matter to God."

This man is happy. He has many bags of cotton, and they are all sheltered under his canopy. The women are returning from the fields, where they have picked lots of millet. A worker is putting away bushels of millet in the man's attic for safekeeping. He is climbing a Mafa ladder to reach the opening. The straw is stored separately on a drying rack.

34 The Guests at the Feast

Matthew 22:1–10 / Luke 14:15–24

Jesus told this parable: "Once a man cooked a great feast and invited many people to come and share it. When it was time for the party, he sent his servant to tell the people he invited: 'Come! Everything is ready now.' But one by one, they all began to give reasons why they couldn't make it. The first one said, 'I just bought some land, and I need to go look at it. I can't make it to the party.' Another one said, 'I just bought some oxen, and I have to go try them out. I can't come.' And someone else said, 'I just got married, so I can't come either.'

"The servant went back to his master and told him all this. The master got angry and said, 'Go out right now into the streets and alleys of town and invite everyone you can find who is poor or blind or disabled.' The servant did it, and then said, 'Sir, all of those people have come, and we still have room for more.' And so the master said, 'Go out to the back roads and get even more people. Fill my house with people! None of the people who were invited first will get a taste of this great feast.'"

In this large **concession**, where clusters of corn hang from the trees, a wealthy man greets a beggar, while an old woman smiles at the idea of filling her calabash. As the man toward the back plays his tam-tam (a type of West African drum), people settle down to rest and drink together from the same cup as a sign of friendship. *Fufu* cooks on the fire, and soon it will be shared and eaten quickly.

The kingdom of God is like a feast where everyone is invited. God sends his messengers out to the highways that lead to the whole world. They are often turned away. Those who have nothing are the first to believe that they will be filled in God's kingdom.

Concession: the enclosed space between the various huts that make up a person's home

35 The Parable of the Prodigal Son

Luke 15:11–24

Jesus told this parable: "There was a man who had two sons. The younger son said to his father, 'Give me my share of the inheritance.' When he got it, he packed his things and left for a faraway country. Then he wasted all his money on wild living. When it was all gone, a terrible famine struck that country and he had nothing to eat for a long time. So he got a job feeding pigs at a nearby farm. He was so hungry, he watched the pigs eating their food and wished he could eat with them.

"He thought to himself, 'The people who work for my father have enough food to eat. But here I am, starving. I'm going to go home to my father and say, "Father, I have sinned against God and against you. I don't even deserve to be called your son. Just treat me like one of your workers."' And he left and headed for home. While he was still a long way off, his father saw him coming and his heart overflowed with love for his son. He ran to him, hugged him tight, and kissed him. The son said, 'Father, I have sinned against God and against you. I don't even deserve to be called your son.'

"But his father told his servants, 'Quick, go find the nicest robe I have and put it on him. Put a ring on his finger and sandals on his feet. Get the fattened calf and cook it. We are going to have a celebration feast because this son of mine was dead, and now he's alive again! He was lost, and now he's found!' And the great celebration began."

In a field where there are still a few stalks of millet standing, the father runs to meet his son. The Mafa people decided that the **prodigal** son's mother should also be here along with the father, and we see her embracing her son, too. All come running, surprised and happy. A little girl is ringing some bells. A servant brings a new garment. The older brother arrives from a distance and is unsure of what is going on.

This is a parable of mercy and forgiveness. In the Lord's Prayer, we ask to receive this forgiveness too, and to give it generously to people who have hurt us.

Prodigal: to give things away carelessly or foolishly

36 The Rich Man and Poor Lazarus

Luke 16:19–31

Jesus told this parable: "Once there was a man who was very rich. He dressed in beautiful clothes and ate big, delicious meals every day. Meanwhile a poor man named Lazarus sat in the street outside his house, covered with sores. Lazarus was so hungry, he would have loved to have been able to eat the crumbs that fell off the rich man's table. Dogs even came and licked his sores.

"When Lazarus died, angels came and carried him to heaven. When the rich man died, he went to hell and suffered terribly. He could see **Abraham** far away in heaven, and Lazarus was with him. He cried out, 'Father Abraham, help me! Send Lazarus to dip his finger in water and cool my tongue with a few drops, because I am in awful pain in this fire.' Abraham replied, 'My son, remember all the good things you had during your lifetime, and how little Lazarus had. Now he is comforted here, while you are suffering.'"

Sitting in the shade of a drying rack under a papaya tree, the rich man is served his food and drink. In the background, shepherds are watching over the man's flocks. In his concession, a woman is busy **threshing** his millet, another refills his water reserves, and his children play. No one thinks of poor Lazarus but the dogs.

Abraham: a man called by God in the Old Testament to start the Jewish faith; he is called "father Abraham" by Jews because he was one of the first to believe in God
Threshing: separating the grains from the rest of a plant; this is done by the Mafa by shaking the harvested millet over a basket, so that the part that is good for cooking and eating goes into the basket while the husks and straw fly away in the wind

37 The Merciless Servant

Matthew 18:23–35

Jesus told this parable: "There was a man who owed a huge amount of money to his master. Since he couldn't pay it back, his master ordered him, his wife, their children, and all his property to be sold to pay off the debt. The servant fell on his knees in front of his master and begged him, 'Please give me more time! I promise I will pay back everything I owe you.' The master felt sorry for the man and canceled the debt.

"When that servant left, he found one of the other servants who owed him just a little bit of money. He grabbed him and started to choke him, yelling, 'Pay me what you owe me!' Falling to his knees, the other man begged him, 'Please give me more time! I promise I will pay back everything I owe you.' But the first man refused. Instead, he had him thrown in jail until he paid back every bit that he owed.

"When the master heard about this, he told the first servant, 'You evil servant! I canceled everything you owed me because you begged me to. Why couldn't you show the same kindness to the other servant?' Then in anger the master had him thrown in jail until he could pay back every bit that he owed.

"That is how my Father in heaven will treat you, unless you forgive people from your heart."

38 The Ten People with Leprosy

Luke 17:11–19

As Jesus entered a village, ten people with **leprosy** came out to meet him. They begged him, "Jesus, help us!" Jesus told them, "Go show yourselves to the priests."

While they were on their way to the priests, their leprosy was healed. When one of the people—who was a Samaritan—saw that he was healed, he immediately turned back, praising God in a loud voice. He went to Jesus and thanked him joyfully. Jesus said, "Weren't ten people healed? Where are the other nine? Was this foreigner the only one to come back and give praise to God?" And he said to the man, "Go home now. Your faith has saved you."

In Jesus's time, people with leprosy were required to stay far away from everyone else to make sure they would not get anyone else sick.

Overjoyed, the people Jesus has healed of leprosy throw their crutches in the air and happily take off their bandages and the special shoes they had to wear. The children who are there watching the scene share their joy. With a smile, Jesus shows he is happy that they have all been healed, but he also knows that nine of them are ungrateful.

In the background, a hut is under construction. Soon its roof will be built.

Leprosy: a contagious skin disease (also called Hansen's Disease) that causes sores to grow on a person's face and arms and legs

39 The Pharisee and the Tax Collector

Luke 18:9–14

Jesus met some people who were sure they were closer to God than anyone else. He told them this parable: "Two people went to the Temple to pray. One was a Pharisee, and the other one was a **tax collector**. The Pharisee stood up near the front of the Temple and prayed, 'O God, thank you for making me better than other people, who steal and lie and commit adultery—like that tax collector back there. I fast twice a week, and I give money to the Temple.'

"The tax collector stood near the back of the Temple. He would not even look up to heaven, but beat his chest and prayed, 'O God, have mercy on me, a sinner.'

"I tell you, the tax collector went home right with God, but the Pharisee did not. Because everyone who thinks highly of himself will be humbled, and those who humble themselves will be raised up."

The Pharisee, in the foreground, is proud that he is an expert in the Jewish religion. Some Pharisees (like Nicodemus in chapter 14) were sincere, but some only wanted to be admired, and this made Jesus sad. Tax collectors like the man in the back were hated by many people because they were very often dishonest. Jesus loved when the tax collector came to humbly ask for forgiveness.

Tax collector: a person whose job was to collect taxes from people for the Roman empire; they often collected more than they were supposed to and kept the extra for themselves

40 Jesus and the Children

Matthew 19:13–15 / Mark 10:13–16 / Luke 18:15–17

People brought their children to Jesus. The disciples tried to keep them away, but Jesus told them to stop. "Let the children come to me," he said. "The kingdom of God belongs to people like them." And he took the children in his arms and blessed them.

In the distance, women are busy making baskets and carrying water. To clean the water, it is passed through a filter, like the one we see on the right side of the image. In the background, we see the Mandara Mountains of northern Cameroon.

Little children long for tenderness. They ask questions because they know that they do not know. They trust. They are humble. Jesus loves them and he wants all people to follow their example.

41 The Workers Who Arrived Last

Matthew 20:1–16

Jesus told this parable: "The kingdom of heaven is like a field where some workers were hired early in the morning, to work for a specific amount of money. Later the landowner found more people to work, and then still more people even later in the day. When the workday was over, he paid the first workers their money, and then paid the same amount to the other workers who came later, even those who started at the end of the day. The first workers asked, 'Why are you paying them the same amount you paid us?'

"The owner said, 'My friend, I'm not cheating you. Didn't I pay you what I promised? Take your money and go. Can't I do what I want with my own money? Are you jealous because I'm generous?'"

And Jesus said, "The people who are last on earth will be first with God, and the people who are first on earth will be last with God."

In this scene, we see the workers in a millet field, where the first group has been working since the early morning under a very hot sun. The landowner is now hiring a second group.

Through this parable, Jesus teaches us that it is never too late for anyone to answer God's call. The workers who started earlier in the morning want to be paid according to the way they expect. But in the kingdom of heaven, God will reward us according to his justice and mercy.

42 The Ten Bridesmaids

Matthew 25:1–13

Jesus said, "The kingdom of heaven will be like ten bridesmaids who took their lamps and went out to wait for the groom. But the groom was late, and the women fell asleep waiting for him. At midnight, the groom finally arrived, but some of the women had forgotten to bring extra oil for their lamps and so they ran out. The ones who brought their own oil didn't have enough for those who didn't, so the others had to go and buy more. Meanwhile, the groom arrived and the wedding banquet started, and those who had to go to buy more oil got locked out."

Jesus said, "Be ready. You never know exactly when the groom"—meaning himself—"will return."

Just like the lamps in Jesus's parable, the kerosene lamps that the Mafa use for light have oil inside, and a wick inside it soaks up the oil and burns slowly. When the oil runs out, the wick goes out and can't burn anymore.

43 The Raising of Lazarus

John 11:1–45

Martha and Mary sent a message to Jesus, saying, "Lord, our brother **Lazarus** is sick." Jesus loved Lazarus and his sisters. But when he heard Lazarus was sick, he waited two days before going to see him. Then he said to his disciples, "Our friend Lazarus has died. But it's good for you that I was not there before, so that now you will believe in me. Let's go."

When Martha heard that Jesus was arriving, she went out to meet him. She told him, "Lord, if you had been here, my brother would not have died. But I know that even now God will do whatever you ask."

Jesus said to her, "I am the resurrection and the life. Whoever believes in me, even if they die, will live." He went out with Martha and Mary to Lazarus's tomb, and when they got there, Jesus cried. Then he said, "Take the stone away from the entrance to the tomb." And he looked toward heaven and prayed, "Father, I thank you for hearing me." And then he shouted loudly, "Lazarus, come out!" And the dead man came out with his hands, feet, and face wrapped in burial cloths. "Unwrap him from the cloths and let him go," Jesus said.

Many Jews who were with the two sisters just before the great Passover feast watched Jesus perform this miracle. From that moment on, the Jewish authorities were afraid of how popular he was, and they decided to find a way to kill him.

Lazarus: a name that comes from the Hebrew word *azar*, which means "someone whom God helps"

44 Zacchaeus

Luke 19:1–10

On the way to Jerusalem, Jesus passed through a town called Jericho. A rich tax collector who lived there, named Zacchaeus, wanted to see Jesus. But he was too short to see over the other people in the crowd. So as Jesus came down the road, he ran ahead and climbed a tall tree. When Jesus was passing by, he looked up the tree and said, "Zacchaeus, come down quickly. I want to visit your house today." So Zacchaeus climbed down and joyfully welcomed Jesus to his home.

When the people saw this, they whispered to each other, "Jesus is going to a sinner's house!" But Zacchaeus told Jesus, "Lord, I'm going to give half of everything I have to the poor, and if I have taken anyone's money unfairly, I will repay four times more than I took."

And Jesus said, "Today salvation has come to this house. This man is a true descendant of Abraham. The Son of Man has come to find people who are lost and save them."

45 The Parable of the Talents

Matthew 25:14–30 / Luke 19:12–27

Jesus said, "Here is another parable about the kingdom of heaven. A man was going on a trip. He called in his servants and put each of them in charge of some of his money. He gave five **talents** to one servant, two talents to another servant, and one talent to a third servant. Then he left. The servant who got five talents traded them and made five more. The one who got two talents traded them and made another two. But the one who got one talent dug a hole in the ground and hid it.

"When the master got back from his trip, he said to the first servant, 'Well done, my good and faithful servant. Since you were reliable with small matters, I will put you in charge of bigger things. Come and share your master's joy!' Then he said the same thing to the second servant. But to the third servant, the master said, 'You evil, lazy servant! I could have put my money in the bank and got some interest for it.' And he took his one talent and gave it to the servant with ten. 'Everyone who does something with their talent will receive more and end up with more than enough. But anyone who doesn't will lose even what he has. Throw that good-for-nothing servant out of my house.'"

God has entrusted each of us with our own talents, gifts, and abilities. We are responsible to develop what we have to help others and make our world better.

Talent: a valuable coin in Jesus's time that was worth thirty pounds of silver

46 Palm Branches

Matthew 20:17–19; 21:1–11 / Mark 10:32–34; 11:1–10 / Luke 18:31–34; 19:28–40 / John 12:12–19

It was almost time for the great Jewish feast of Passover. Jesus told his apostles, "We are going to Jerusalem. There the Son of Man will be mocked and insulted and spit on. They will kill him, but on the third day he will rise." But the apostles had no idea what he was talking about.

Five days before Passover, Jesus entered Jerusalem riding on the back of a donkey. Crowds of people came to welcome him. They cheered and praised God and laid down palm branches along his path. Some Pharisees in the crowd said to him, "Teacher, tell your disciples to stop this." And he said, "If the people were quiet, the stones would shout instead."

The beat of the drums accompanies the shouts of the crowd. In the distance, someone beats out a tune on an instrument that looks like a large box, used only at special times. People spread out blankets in front of Jesus on his path. Women are dancing and children are jumping happily. Jesus knows that another crowd will soon condemn him to death. From this time on, the religious leaders worried about who was in charge because so many Jews wanted to follow Jesus.

47 Jesus Chases Out the Money Changers

Matthew 21:12–13 / Mark 11:15–17 / Luke 19:45–46 / John 2:13–22

Once they were in Jerusalem, Jesus went to the temple. When he saw all the people in the temple area selling oxen, sheep, and doves, and business people exchanging money, he became very angry. He made a whip out of ropes and chased all the merchants and all their animals out of the temple area. He knocked over their tables and hurled their coins all over the ground.

"Get out of here!" Jesus yelled. "Don't you dare make my Father's house into a marketplace!"

There was a market set up around the temple where the Jews could buy birds, sheep, and even oxen to offer to God as a sacrifice. To buy something, they had to exchange for the kinds of money that were accepted inside the temple area. This explains why the money changers were there.

Jesus was probably seeing all the market people in the temple area for the first time. Not long before this, they had to set up their stores farther away from the sacred space.

And so he showed his love for this holy and beautiful building, the temple of God his Father. When the Jews asked him, "What sign can you give us?" he replied, "Destroy this Temple, and in three days I will raise it back up." Later, after Jesus's resurrection, the disciples understood that he had been talking about the temple of his body.

48 The Widow's Gift

Mark 12:41–44 / Luke 21:1–4

Jesus stood near the temple, watching the box where people put their donations. He saw many rich people putting in lots of money. Then a poor widow came by and dropped in two copper coins, not worth very much. He pointed her out to his disciples and said, "That poor widow gave more than anyone else. The rich gave from what they had left over, but she gave all she had to live on."

As the Mafa villagers were preparing to stage this scene for the artist to paint, a young woman came forward with her child. Everyone started saying, "She's a real widow. She's the one who should represent the widow in the parable!" And so she did.

49 Jesus Washes Peter's Feet

John 13:3–20

In Jerusalem, Jesus ate a Passover meal with his apostles. While they sat at the table together, he got up, took off his outer clothes, and wrapped a towel around his waist. Then he poured water into a large bowl and washed each of his apostles' feet. He dried them with the towel around his waist. When he got to Peter, he said to Jesus, "Lord, I can't let you wash my feet." But Jesus told him, "You will understand later why I want to."

Then he said to them all, "Do you realize what I have done for you? You call me 'teacher' and 'master,' and you're right, because that's what I am. So if I, your teacher and master, wash your feet, you need to wash each other's feet. I have given you a model to follow. What I did, you must do."

Jesus reaches out for Peter's feet, but Peter pulls them away and raises his hands, refusing to let Jesus wash them. At the time, washing the feet of travelers who had walked barefoot or in sandals along the dusty roads was a way of welcoming a guest, and was supposed to be done by a servant or slave. Peter loves and admires Jesus, so he doesn't want him to do something that a servant should do. In those days, no one would think of doing any kind of work that they were too important to do.

50 The Last Supper

Matthew 26:26–30 / Mark 14:22–26 / Luke 22:14–20 / 1 Corinthians 11:23–26

At that same Passover meal, while they were eating, Jesus picked up bread, he said a prayer of thanks for it, and he broke it. Then he gave it to his disciples and said, "Take this and eat it. This is my body." Then he took a cup of wine, he said a prayer of thanks for it, and he gave it to them. He said, "All of you drink from it. This is my blood of the new **covenant**, which I will pour out to forgive people's sins. I will not drink wine again until I drink it with you in my Father's kingdom." Then they sang a hymn together and went out to the Mount of Olives.

The meal in the picture is a feast. One of the apostles gently strikes his tam-tam, and there is a small stringed instrument on the ground beside it. They are about to sing, before heading out for the Mount of Olives.

The Mafa do not have bread or wine. Their "bread" is *fufu*; they also drink a beer made from millet, which we see here in a beautiful and large calabash. Meanwhile, Judas looks away. He will be the disciple who betrays Jesus and turns him over to the people who want to kill him.

At every moment of every day, and all over the world, thousands of celebrations of the Eucharist take place.

Covenant: a special oath between God and God's people that establishes bonds like a family's

51 Gethsemane

Matthew 26:30–46 / Mark 14:26–42 / Luke 22:39–46 / John 18:1

After the meal, Jesus and his apostles walked to the Mount of Olives, to a garden called Gethsemane. Jesus said to his disciples, "Sit here while I go over there and pray," but he brought Peter, James, and John up with him. Jesus became very upset and said to them, "My soul is nearly sad to death. Please stay here and wait with me." He walked a little farther into the garden, then fell with his face to the ground and prayed, "Father, if it is possible, let me not have to drink this cup of suffering. But let not what I want happen, but what you want."

Then he walked back to his disciples and saw that they were sleeping. He said to Peter, "Couldn't you even wait with me for one hour? Pray that you will not be tested as I am about to be tested. The spirit is willing, but the body is weak."

Jesus walked back to where he was before and he prayed again, "Father, if I have to drink this cup of suffering, then may what you want be done!" He went back to his disciples and saw that they were asleep again because they were too tired to keep their eyes open. He went back a third time and prayed the same prayer again. Then he returned to his disciples and said to them, "You're still sleeping? Look! It is time for the Son of Man to be handed over to sinners. Get up. Here comes the person who will hand me over to them."

52 Judas's Kiss

Matthew 26:47–56 / Mark 14:43–50 / Luke 22:47–53 / John 18:3–12

While Jesus was still speaking, one of his apostles, Judas, arrived along with a group of soldiers. They had planned that Judas would give them a sign. He had told them, "Arrest the man that I kiss."

Judas walked right over to Jesus and gave him a kiss. "My friend," Jesus said, "are you betraying the Son of Man with a kiss?" Then Jesus said to the soldiers, "Why have you come after me like I'm some criminal? I sat teaching in the Temple area every day, and you didn't arrest me then. But everything is happening to fulfill what the prophets said would happen." When Jesus's apostles saw him being arrested, they all ran away and hid.

In this image, we see Jesus, Judas, and the soldiers standing in a forest of teak trees because there are no olive trees in northern Cameroon like the ones we read about in the Gospels.

53 Peter Denies Jesus

Matthew 26:69–75 / Mark 14:66–72 / Luke 22:54–62 / John 18:17, 25–27

After the soldiers arrested Jesus, they took him to the high priest. While the high priest questioned Jesus, Peter waited outside by a fire that some other people had built. One of the people noticed Peter and said, "This man was with Jesus." But Peter said, "No I wasn't. I don't even know that man." A little later, someone else saw Peter and said, "You are one of Jesus's friends." But Peter said, "I am not." And an hour after that, still another person said, "This man must be one of his disciples, because he's a Galilean like Jesus." And Peter got angry and said, "I don't even know what you're talking about!"

And just as he said that, a rooster crowed and Peter remembered that Jesus had told him, "Before the rooster crows tonight, you will pretend you don't even know me three times." Peter was very sad that he had lied about knowing Jesus, and he walked away crying.

Peter is afraid because the guards have noticed his Galilean accent. They stare at him suspiciously and then accuse him of being Jesus's follower. He denies it. Meanwhile, in the background, we see an angry crowd surrounding Jesus. And on the bottom left, we see a rooster perched on his branch.

54 Jesus Is Scourged

Matthew 27:11–26 / Mark 15:2–15 / John 18:29—19:1

Jesus was brought to the Roman governor, named Pilate. It was a tradition that the governor could release one prisoner each year on Passover. So Pilate asked the crowd of people, "What do you want me to do with Jesus?"

And they shouted back, "Crucify him!"

"But he didn't do anything wrong," Pilate said.

And they shouted again, "Crucify him!"

Pilate took a bowl of water and washed his hands in front of the crowd, saying, "This man's death will not be my fault. It will be yours!" He sent Jesus to be scourged and crucified, and let another criminal, named Barabbas, go free.

As Roman governor of the region where Jesus lived, Pontius Pilate had the power to punish criminals however he wanted. Often, people found guilty of crimes were sentenced to scourging, which was a painful beating with a whip made of leather straps with balls of lead on the end.

In Turin, Italy, there is a cloth that some people think was the shroud used to wrap Jesus's body after he died. It has a mysterious image of a crucified body with more than a hundred bloody wounds from scourging.

55 The Crucifixion

Matthew 27:32–54 / Mark 15:20–39 / Luke 23:33–46 / John 19:16–37

The soldiers brought Jesus to the place called Golgotha. There they nailed his hands and feet to a cross. Jesus prayed, "Father, forgive them. They don't understand what they are doing."

Two criminals were crucified with him. While they hung on their three crosses together, one of them made fun of Jesus, saying, "Aren't you supposed to be the Messiah? Save yourself, and us, too!" But the other criminal told him to stop. He said, "Aren't you afraid of making God angry? You and I are getting what we deserve. But this man didn't hurt anyone." And he turned to Jesus and said, "Jesus, please remember me when you are in your kingdom."

Jesus said to him, "Today you will be with me in heaven."

On the ground below the cross where Jesus was hanging, his mother Mary stood along with her sister and Mary Magdalene, who was one of Jesus's disciples. Jesus looked at his mother and his disciple John who was also standing nearby, and he said to his mother, "This is your son now." And then he said to John, "This is your mother now."

The sky was dark from noon until three o'clock, while Jesus hung dying on the cross. Around three o'clock, he cried out, "My God, my God, why have you left me all alone?" Then the ground shook and the big curtain in the temple suddenly tore down the middle. And Jesus cried out, "Father, I give you back my spirit." And he hung his head and died.

A soldier who was standing there watching became upset and scared, and he said, "This man was definitely the Son of God!"

The painful crown of thorns that the soldiers wove together and put on Jesus's head was to make fun of him because some people had called him a king.

56 The Resurrection

"The last enemy to be defeated will be death" (1 Corinthians 15:26).

"I am the resurrection and the life" (John 11:25).

"The Son of Man must suffer much and be rejected by the elders, chief priests, and the teachers of the Law. He will be put to death, but three days later he will be raised to life" (Luke 9:22).

"Why are you looking among the dead for one who is alive? He is not here, he has been raised" (Luke 24:5–6).

"If Christ has not yet been raised from death, then we have nothing to preach and you have nothing to believe" (1 Corinthians 15:14).

"God has raised this very Jesus from death, and we are all witnesses to the fact" (Acts 2:32).

No one saw the resurrection of Christ, but many artists have tried to represent it, often with strong images and bold colors. But in reality, this event was not dazzling and loud; it was invisible and mysterious. Here the artist imagines it happening in the early morning—the night is coming to an end and the sky is pink as daylight approaches. Palm trees, which are symbols of life, surround the risen Jesus, and the light of dawn reflects brightly on the loose strips of Jesus's burial shroud. Christ escapes the kingdom of death and rises into the light. He is the Light. He is Life.

57 The Women at the Tomb

Matthew 28:1–10 / Mark 16:1–8 / Luke 24:1–11 / John 20:1–10

On Sunday, at sunrise, Mary, Mary Magdalene, and Salome went to the tomb where Jesus had been buried because they wanted to anoint his body. One of the women said, "Who will roll away the big stone in front of the tomb, so that we can go in?" But when they got there, they saw that the stone was already rolled away. When they stepped inside the tomb, they saw an angel dressed in white sitting there, and they were terrified.

The angel said to the women, "Do not be afraid. You are looking for Jesus, the one they crucified, but he is not here. He is risen! Look here at the place where they laid his body. So go now, and tell his apostles!"

58 Jesus Appears to Mary Magdalene

John 20:11–18

Mary Magdalene was outside Jesus's tomb crying. She turned around and saw Jesus standing there, but she did not know it was him. She thought he was the gardener. Jesus said to her, "Woman, why are you crying? Who are you looking for?" Mary said to him, "Sir, if you took Jesus's body, please tell me where you put it, and I will take it." Then Jesus said, "Mary!" And suddenly she recognized him and cried, "Rabbi!"

Jesus said to her, "Don't hold on to me, because I have not returned yet to my Father. But go to the people who believe in me and tell them I am going to my Father and your Father, to my God and your God." And so Mary ran to the disciples and told them, "I have seen the Lord!"

59 On the Way to Emmaus

Mark 16:12–13 / Luke 24:13–35

That same day, two of Jesus's disciples were walking together to a town called Emmaus. It was a two-hour walk from Jerusalem. While they walked, they talked about all the things that had happened. And a man came along and began to walk with them. It was Jesus, but they didn't recognize him.

Jesus asked them, "What were you talking about?" One of them, named Cleopas, said, "You must be the only person who doesn't know about the things that happened in Jerusalem these last few days." And Jesus asked, "What things?"

They said, "The things that happened to Jesus of Nazareth. He was a mighty prophet, but our chief priests and leaders handed him over for a death sentence and he was nailed to a cross. We were hoping he would be the one to set our people free.

"Now today is the third day since he died, and some women in our group are saying they went to his tomb early this morning and found it empty. They came back talking about seeing an angel who said he is alive. Some of us went and checked it out, and just like they said, he was gone, and they couldn't find the body."

Jesus said, "Why is this so hard for you to understand? Didn't the prophets say the Messiah would need to suffer so that he could enter into glory?" And then, starting from the stories of Moses, Jesus talked about all the verses in the scriptures that were about him. As they got near the town, he acted like he was going to keep on walking. But the disciples talked him into staying with them.

When they sat down to eat supper, Jesus picked up bread, said a prayer of thanks for it, broke it, and gave it to them. That was when the disciples realized it was Jesus, and suddenly he disappeared.

It's a night like any other at a little inn far from any town or village. Women prepare a meal, feed their babies, and send a little girl to bring their customers more to drink. As the two men recognize Christ, one of them stands up, amazed and surprised. The other one believes and begins to pray, extending his hands. The disciples will run back to Jerusalem to join the apostles and form the new church.

60 Thomas

John 20:24–29

The apostle named Thomas was not with the rest of the apostles when the risen Jesus came to them the first time. When Thomas got back, they told him, "We have seen the Lord!" But he didn't believe them. He said, "I won't believe it until I can touch the nail marks in his hands and put my finger in his side where the soldier pierced him with a spear."

A week later, the apostles were together again, and this time Thomas was there, too. Jesus came to them again, even though the doors were locked. He stood with them and said, "Peace be with you." And he went to Thomas and said, "Here, Thomas. Touch the nail marks in my hands. Put your finger in my side. Don't doubt anymore, but believe."

Thomas said, "My Lord and my God!"

Jesus told him, "You believe now because you saw me. Blessed are the people who believe even though they will never be able to see me."

61 Sent on a Mission

Matthew 28:16–20 / Mark 16:14–18

The apostles went to Galilee, and Jesus appeared to them there. When they saw him, they worshiped him, but they also doubted.

Jesus told them, “God has given me all power in heaven and earth. I am sending you to go and help people all over the world become my disciples. Baptize them in the name of the Father, and of the Son, and of the Holy Spirit. Teach them to do everything I have taught you. And you can be sure that I will be with you forever.”

The huge landscape in the background shows how big is the mission of bringing the good news about Jesus to the world. We see the apostles heading out, two by two. Some are already starting to talk to the first people they meet in the village.

The apostles of Jesus made their way to Rome, Spain, Greece, Ethiopia, Egypt, and as far away as Persia and India. All of them spent the rest of their lives sharing the good news of Christ, and most of them died for it.

62 The Ascension of Jesus

Mark 16:19 / Luke 24:50–53 / Acts 1:9–11

Jesus led his disciples out toward the town of Bethany, and he told them, "You will receive power from the Holy Spirit, and you will be my witnesses throughout the whole world." Then he raised his hands and blessed them. And as he blessed them, he was taken up to heaven.

Although the Gospel story does not say one way or the other, the Mafa people included Jesus's mother with the apostles when Jesus ascended. They made sure she was at Pentecost, too.

63 Pentecost

Acts 2:1–13

Fifty days after Jesus rose from the dead, all the apostles were together in one place. Suddenly a loud noise like a blowing wind filled the entire house they were in. Then fire appeared in the air over them. The flames separated and tongues of fire came to land on each of the apostles' heads. And they were all filled with the Holy Spirit. They all started speaking in different languages that they didn't know how to speak before, which the Spirit gave them the ability to do.

There were faithful Jewish people from all over the world in Jerusalem that day because they had all come to celebrate Passover. When they heard the sound of all this happening, a big crowd gathered in the city. But they were amazed and confused because every person heard the apostles speaking in their own language.

The Apostle Paul later wrote to the Christians in Corinth: "There are various gifts, but it's the same spirit. There are various ways to serve, but it's the same Lord. All of you are the body of Christ and each one of you is a part of this body" (see 1 Corinthians 12:4–13). That means that some people will teach about God through prayer, others through teaching out loud, others by the loving ways they live, others by their family life. All who are baptized have different roles, but together they form the Church of Jesus Christ.

We see the apostles have locked themselves in a Mafa building full of fishing equipment. We can see in all their faces the ways they react to the call of the Holy Spirit—some with outward joy and others with a quieter, inner joy. A couple of them are scared and huddling together because they understand that this call will mean accepting a mission that could lead them to giving up their very lives. Full of action, John is already on the move. Another disciple, to the right, is grabbing hold of his seat, unable to believe what is happening. Near him, Jesus's mother makes a gesture of welcoming—she had said yes to God before and now she's doing it again. An older apostle, dazzled, takes hold of his walking staff. Another apostle on his knees expresses his complete confidence and adoration. Yet another has opened the door. Peter, who is holding a calabash, stops drinking—it's time to get going.

Stunned and confused by the words of the apostles, the crowd will ask, "What does all this mean? Have they been drinking too much?" "No," Peter will answer. "See, our calabashes are still full because it's only nine o'clock in the morning!"

The Virgin of Brin (named for a village in the Casamance region of Senegal)

Mary, Door of Heaven